Merry Christmas

You are always my daughter

You are always loved everyday

You are prayed for each morning

Keep Thriving

I love you always
Mom

Rebecca C Walker

Merry Christmas
Michelle

We are sending my
daughter
we are asking her
everyday
we are hoping for
good morning

Keep driving
it was fun going
Now

Sign I need

Get What You Want

The 3 Keys for Creating Your Thriving Business and Life

Rebecca C Wilcox

Special **FREE** Bonus Gift for You!

To help you achieve more success, there are **FREE BONUS RESOURCES FOR YOU** at:

www.FreeGiftFromRebecca.com

Copyright © 2023 Lawson & Cobb, Inc.
ALL RIGHTS RESERVED

No part of this book or its associated ancillary materials may be reproduced or transmitted in any form or by any means, electronic or mechanical, including photocopying, recording, or by any informational storage or retrieval system without permission from the publisher.

PUBLISHED BY: Lawson & Cobb, Inc.

DISCLAIMER AND/OR LEGAL NOTICES
While all attempts have been made to verify information provided in this book and its ancillary materials, neither the author or publisher assumes any responsibility for errors, inaccuracies or omissions and is not responsible for any financial loss by customer in any manner. Any slights of people or organizations are unintentional. If advice concerning legal, financial, accounting or related matters is needed, the services of a qualified professional should be sought. This book and its associated ancillary materials, including verbal and written training, is not intended for use as a source of legal, financial or accounting advice. You should be aware of the various laws governing business transactions or other business practices in your particular geographical location.

EARNINGS & INCOME DISCLAIMER
With respect to the reliability, accuracy, timeliness, usefulness, adequacy, completeness, and/ or suitability of information provided in this book, Rebecca C Wilcox, Lawson & Cobb, Inc., its partners, associates, affiliates, consultants, and/or presenters make no warranties, guarantees, representations, or claims of any kind. Readers' results will vary depending on a number of

factors. Any and all claims or representations as to income earnings are not to be considered as average earnings. Testimonials are not representative. This book and all products and services are for educational and informational purposes only. Use caution and see the advice of qualified professionals. Check with your accountant, attorney or professional advisor before acting on this or any information. You agree that Rebecca C Wilcox and/or Lawson & Cobb, Inc. is not responsible for the success or failure of your personal, business, health or financial decisions relating to any information presented by Rebecca C Wilcox, Lawson & Cobb, Inc.., or company products/services. Earnings potential is entirely dependent on the efforts, skills and application of the individual person. Any examples, stories, references, or case studies are for illustrative purposes only and should not be interpreted as testimonies and/or examples of what reader and/or consumers can generally expect from the information. No representation in any part of this information, materials and/or seminar training are guarantees or promises for actual performance. Any statements, strategies, concepts, techniques, exercises and ideas in the information, materials and/or seminar training offered are simply opinion or experience, and thus should not be misinterpreted as promises, typical results or guarantees (expressed or implied). The author and publisher (Rebecca C Wilcox, Lawson & Cobb, Inc., (RCW) or any of RCW's representatives) shall in no way, under any circumstances, be held liable to any party (or third party) for any direct, indirect, punitive, special, incidental or other consequential damages arising directly or indirectly from any use of books, materials and or seminar trainings, which is provided "as is," and without warranties.

What Others Are Saying About Rebecca Wilcox and Her Strategies

"The coaching journey with Rebecca has changed my life by helping my entire outlook on life become more positive by managing my expectations of my day, being a stronger person and motivating me to finish daily activities. With Rebecca's coaching I gained confidence and became a stronger person that I knew I could be. I received help with motivational strategies to improve myself."

- **Teresa McCauley,** Caregiver and Writer

"Having Rebecca as my coach who was committed to my success even when my life started going haywire, was the anchor I needed to keep believing I could do greater things in my life."

- **Betsy Fulmer,** Art Teacher

"Rebecca, I just want to thank you for always taking the time to validate me as a person. You call out my strengths in our sessions and reflect the passion I have. You have such a high degree of emotional intelligence! I just want to thank you for that! I can't believe how far I've come with your help in just a few months."

- **Elisa Collins,** Founder and CEO Discovery NP Legal Consultants

"Rebecca is an amazing person. I recently went through an activity with her for my self-growth. She was great in how she reflected back to me what I was initially saying and then she would encourage me to dig deeper into myself to discover things about myself that I had not realized before. She was non-judgmental, encouraging, and understanding with the discoveries that were made."

- **Darin Fansler,** CEO Wise Business Consultant Corp.

"Thank you, Rebecca, for the motivation and helping me figure out what my superpower was."

— **Galyn Ferguson,** Client Attraction and Marketing Strategist

"Rebecca guided me through an important exercise I needed to help me move forward with my business. She guided me thought it so effectively, seamlessly and with great insight. Rebecca cares deeply for the person she works with and I would recommend her in a heart beat."

— **Johanne Aube,** Business Coach

"Rebecca helped me with clarity, confidence and being ready for the opportunities God presents. Rebecca shared her wisdom to give grace to myself while I strive for excellence."

— **Shanna Harris,** Master Life Coach at Spirit Goals

"I have listened to Rebecca share her strategies on starting your day and can testify that once you have heard her message, you don't forget it! What was so life-changing for me is the realization that by nurturing the way I start each day; I am setting an important foundation in place. Thank you for investing such important insights for us."

- **Julie Brown,** Author, Coach, Speaker, and Founder of The Proverbs 31 Movement

"You are an outstanding listener and I love the fact that your experience and creativity lend authority to the responses you give. You encouraged me to take what I learned and mold it into something I could use. You are a very giving, wise and loving teacher and you want to help your students succeed."

- **Marquina Rawlings,** Owner and CEO Studio Marquina, LLC

"I love having a dedicated time to dream out loud with Rebecca and talk through gray areas. She has wonderful business and client service experience. Her knowledge in the online social selling space has been very beneficial as well! She has contacts that she has connected me with... her coaching program has been incredibly beneficial in so many more ways than expected! Going through Rebecca's program encouraged me to take time to slow down and write out my goals, really thinking about what I want to do and map out the steps I need to get there."

- **Christina Proctor,** Wellness Entrepreneur and Business Coach

"A major insight I had during coaching with Rebecca was being able to be more in control of my time."

- **Michele Fisher,** Marketing Strategist

"I would highly recommend Rebecca Wilcox as a coach and mentor. Becky is not just a business Coach. She is a caring person who looks at each client individually and works diligently to help each person grow. I have learned through Becky how to work on my mindset and make it work for me instead of against me. If you want a Coach who is willing to over-deliver and give you the valuable information to move you forward, you want her in your corner."

- **Nancy Lipari,** Relationship Coach, Author, Educator

"Rebecca, I appreciate you so much! You have helped me on my journey of personal growth for almost two years now! You have helped me improve my confidence and I admire your enthusiasm about helping us women discover our power as strong Christian women! Thank you!"

- **Amy Langford,** Dedicated Mother and Friend

"I struggled immensely with negative self-talk and making myself a priority in life. I struggled with getting caught up in the mundane part of life, and I wasn't focusing on why I am here. Sure, I am a wife and mom, but there was a part of me that knew there was MORE. Through coaching with Rebecca, I found that my heart is for mommas and women to know they are not alone in life. And I believe my mission is to express my mess and allow God to turn it into a message."

- **Christina Trusdle,** Natural Living Advocate

"The best thing of this coaching experience with Rebecca was having her encourage me each week, as she walked with me through the darkest days of my life. And I did not give up! She taught me new skills, some of which I've known but haven't used in some time.. Rebecca helped me set goals for myself and to prioritize. And if for some reason I failed at my goal deadline, I just needed to re-adjust my goals. But don't give up!"

- **Linda Jones,** Mary Kaye Consultant

Motivate and Inspire Others!

Retail $24.95

Special Quantity Discounts

5-20 Books	$21.95
21-99 Books	$18.95
100-499 Books	$15.95
500-999 Books	$10.95
1,000+ Books	$8.95

Special Discount Pricing is subject to change.
Please contact us for final pricing options.

To Place an Order Contact:
Rebecca C Wilcox
P.O. Box 707, Arkadelphia, AR 71923
rebecca@rebeccacwilcox.com

The Ideal Professional Speaker for Your Next Event!

Any organization that wants to develop their people to become "extraordinary," needs to hire Rebecca C Wilcox for a keynote and/or workshop training!

To Contact or Book Rebecca C Wilcox to Speak:

rebecca@rebeccacwilcox.com

The Ideal Coach (or Mentor) for You!

If you're ready to overcome challenges, have major breakthroughs and achieve higher levels, then you will love having Rebecca C Wilcox as your coach!

To Contact Rebecca C Wilcox:

rebecca@rebeccacwilcox.com

Dedication

I dedicate this book to my amazing family and dearest friends with the utmost respect, admiration, and sincere appreciation. Without the valuable lessons you have taught me throughout my life, I wouldn't be where I am today, and I am incredibly blessed to have you in my life. I express my heartfelt gratitude to you and want you to know how much I love and cherish you all.

Josephine Cobb – my mother who unconditionally loved me.

Louis Cobb – my father who helped me to understand everyone has their own struggles that cause them to react as they do.

Christine Cobb – my sister who has loved me all our years, gives me support in all areas of my life, and is an exceptional woman who I'm thankful for.

Mike Wilcox – my soulmate, my husband, my lover, and friend. Because of you, I found my voice and confidence to step into the woman I have become. Thank you for your never-ending support and all the laughter you have brought to my life.

Michael, Michelle, and Megan - My precious children have not only grown into incredible adults but also helped me develop a deeper love, patience, and understanding for the intricacies of their unique personalities. Plus, the deep love I have for all my grandchildren they have given me!

To three of my dear friends:

Cheryl Braaten is a beautiful example of what a mother should be, and she helped me navigate motherhood during those early years. She showed me the way with her kind and caring nature, and demonstrated how dear a friend could be.

Teresa McCauley is a woman with immense inner strength and faithfulness as a dear friend. The security of knowing you are always a phone call away means so much to me.

Namron Cesarz is not just my business partner, but also my biggest cheerleader, slot machine playing buddy, and the friend with whom I can laugh into the night. With her by my side, the load of growing our businesses feels much lighter, and I am grateful for her presence in my life.

Table of Contents

Foreword 1

Message to You! 5

What Do You Want and 11
How Can You Get It

Key #1 Ignite **19**

Lock #1 Responsibility 23

Lock #2 Vision Mapping 31

Lock #3 Non-Negotiable Actions 47

Key #2 Refine **55**

Lock #1 Strength 61

Lock #2 Stance 71

Lock #3 Stability 83

Key #3 Evaluate **89**

Lock #1 The Pivot 93

Lock #2 Accountability 101

Lock #3 Celebration 109

One Last Message 115
About Rebecca Wilcox 119
Time Hack Fast Track Accelerator Program 121
References 123

Foreword

The day I first met Rebecca remains vivid in my memory, as I was overcome with a sense of admiration and awe. For quite some time, I had been following her on social media soaking up her wisdom and learning and growing through her insightful posts and engaging videos. To be honest, I think the exact words I used to describe my feelings were "fan-girl."

From the very beginning, it became clear that Rebecca has an incredible gift for forging genuine connections with those around her. Her warmth, compassion, and enthusiasm instantly put me at ease, and our bond seemed to form as naturally as if we had been friends for ages. Little did I know this serendipitous meeting would mark the beginning of an extraordinary friendship and collaboration.

Rebecca's professional journey is nothing short of remarkable. She has successfully owned a brick & mortar store, run a thriving online business, and coached countless professionals in their pursuit of success. Through years of hard work and dedication, she has mastered the skills needed to create a flourishing business and life, and now, she's on a mission to help others achieve the same.

In this book, Rebecca generously shares the keys to her success, offering a powerful and practical strategy that can transform your personal and professional life. Her teachings go beyond theory, as she lives and leads by example, embodying the principles she espouses in her daily life.

As you delve into the pages of this book, you'll be inspired, educated, and empowered by the tools Rebecca has created, and her dedication to helping others reach their full potential. You'll discover the secret to having a thriving business and life and achieving the dreams you've always envisioned.

So, prepare to be enlightened, challenged, and inspired as you embark on this transformative journey with Rebecca as your guide. I have no doubt that the wisdom and guidance you'll find within these pages will change your life for the better, just as it has changed mine.

Namron Cesarz
Business Coach and Consultant

Message to You!

When I was 20 years old, I was about to start my Senior year of college, and my father said something to me that I'll never forget. He told me he didn't have any faith in me, never did, and never would. Growing up, my father was verbally abusive, and as a result, I struggled to form my own opinions and felt like I had to always stay under the radar to avoid his wrath. I just focused on doing well in school and making sure not to bring any dishonor to the family.

My father was always concerned about our family's reputation in society, so I always had to be above reproach. I was scared of him, and I knew that if I did anything that warranted "the look," it was not going to be good. It was tough because I was so close to my mom, and it hurt me deeply whenever she was on the receiving end of my father's verbal abuse. Despite everything, she continued to show me the most unconditional love, and for that, I am forever grateful.

When I look back at that time in my life, I realize that I was given the role model of a subservient wife and a controlling husband. But, as I've grown older and gained more life experience, I've come to understand that this was not how I should live my life.

It has taken me several years to come to the realization that my father's behavior towards me was a reflection of his own upbringing and the tools he had acquired to deal with life's challenges. His impatience, temper, and lack of unconditional love were all developed during his own formative years. I understand that this is not an excuse for his behavior, but it does offer me some perspective.

The biggest difference between my father and myself is that he never believed he should be better. He was content with the tools he had, even if they were not the most effective or healthy. However, I have come to realize that I can break the cycle of negative behavior and strive to be a better person, both for myself and for those around me.

While my relationship with my father may not have been ideal, I have learned valuable lessons from it, and it has shaped the person I am today. I am committed to being a kind, patient, and loving person, and I will continue to work towards that goal every day.

For the longest time, I had a fixed mindset when it came to my intelligence. I believed that I only had a certain amount of intelligence, and if something was too difficult, I would shy away from it because I didn't think I was smart enough to do it. Looking back, I realize that this limiting belief held me back in many aspects of my life.

Growing up, I was never taught how to develop a growth mindset and was never given the tools to realize that I could work harder on something and figure out how to do it. However, this doesn't mean that I didn't accomplish a lot in my life. It wasn't until I turned 60 that I began to examine the value of what I was doing and realized that I had the potential to achieve even more.

Now, I understand that my intelligence is not fixed, and I have the ability to grow and develop my skills through hard work and determination. I have learned to embrace challenges and to view them as opportunities for growth and development, rather than insurmountable obstacles.

While it took me some time to adopt this new mindset, I am grateful for the opportunity to continue learning and growing, no matter my age. And I hope that my journey can inspire others to believe in their own potential and to never stop pursuing their dreams, no matter what challenges they may face.

In 2013, at the age of 57, I made the difficult decision to close my brick-and-mortar store after 25 years of being known as the "feed store lady." While it was a challenging transition, I continued to operate my business online by sending products to Amazon for fulfillment, and I still do this to this day.

As my children had grown and moved on with their lives, I found myself struggling with a sense of identity. I was no longer the hands-on mom that I used to be, and I began to question who I was outside of my role as a business owner and mother.

This period of introspection and self-reflection led me down a path of discovery, as I began to explore my passions and interests beyond my traditional roles. I delved into the world of mindset research and discovered the power of positive thinking and the importance of personal growth and development.

Through this journey, I have come to realize that my identity is not defined by my job title or my role as a mother. I am a multifaceted individual with unique interests and talents, and I am committed to continuing to explore and develop them.

While this period of uncertainty was challenging, it ultimately led me to a deeper sense of self-awareness and a greater appreciation for the value of personal growth and development.

As time went on, I began to feel a strong sense of nudging from God, leading me towards aligning myself with other faith-filled entrepreneurs. It was then that the real fun began. I decided to pursue a Life Coaching certification and began coaching individuals and groups. The joy of watching my clients excel in both their business and personal lives has been incredibly fulfilling, and it has sparked a desire to reach even more women.

As I continue to learn and grow in this field, I find myself increasingly excited about the possibilities that lie ahead. The pursuit of knowledge and personal development has become an enjoyable adventure, and I am grateful for the opportunity to help others along their own journey of growth and transformation.

I believe that with faith, determination, and a willingness to learn and grow, we can all achieve great things. And I am excited to see where this path will lead me next.

What Do You Want and How Can You Get It

If you're anything like me, you've probably wondered how other people manage to get what they want out of life. They seem to have it all together,

while you might be over there struggling to make ends meet. What's their secret?

As it turns out, there is no secret—just a simple process that anyone can follow.

Can you answer "Yes" to any of the following:

- I've tried self-help courses and they never worked.
- I can't add doing one more thing to my day.
- It's too hard to set definite times to do tasks.
- I have children and never know when their needs trump my business needs.

- When I went to a job, I didn't have to worry about all the things I needed to do in running my household during work hours.
- My brain feels like there is too much noise coming in, from social media to emails to growing my business.

If you answered "Yes" to any of those statements, this book is definitely for you!

There are two questions that are simple to ask but not as simple to answer.

- What do you want?
- How can you get it?

"What do you want?" might seem like an obvious question, but it's important to take the time to really think about your answer.

- What do you want out of life?
- What kind of business do you want to create?
- What kind of lifestyle do you want to lead?

Once you have a good understanding of what you want, you can begin to figure out how to make it happen.

The second question of "How can you get it?" is where the rubber meets the road—once you know what you want, it's time to start taking the right steps toward making it a reality.

There is no one-size-fits-all answer to this question, as the best way to achieve your goals will vary depending on what they are. However, there are some general principles you can follow that will help you get started.

After thirty-five years of research and my own personal journey, I can now share with you how to get what you want in easy, fun, and lucrative ways!

Hang in there with me as I tell you a story of the turning point in my life that stopped the chaos and had me stepping into every day being more excited.

It happened! I finally closed my brick-and-mortar store that had been draining my finances and was sucking the life out of my soul. Whew! The weight of carrying this kind of burden was finally lifted, and I felt like hope had been restored to my life.

Now, what did I want? It was time to make a change from how I had been existing, which was just getting by, to extraordinary living with self-love, daily actions, and habits for creating my thriving life!

You see, my life for three years before I closed my brick-and-mortar store consisted of being in a depressed state and knowing I only wanted to:

- Be free from this debt.
- Stop worrying every day about how to pay bills.
- Wake up in the morning thankful for another day.

There was a whole lot of "lack of thinking" going on. Lack thinking is about not believing that I could accomplish something or gain something from my actions. It was all-consuming with every decision I faced, every person I encountered, every dollar that was going down the drain.

But don't get me wrong, I had this business for a total of twenty-five years, it provided for me and my family and was a valuable service to the farming community. For that I was extremely grateful!

However, when things started going downhill, I didn't share this with anyone. Because of that, I didn't have anyone who could offer advice or help.

Why didn't I share my problems with someone else? Here are three reasons:

- What would others think of me?
- How could I deal with disappointing others?
- Everyone would blame me for this failure.

Can you relate to any of those thoughts? They always create a sick feeling in the pit of my stomach!

This type of thinking can keep you stuck in your own kind of hell. But isn't that what limiting beliefs do? They dim your light, your spark, and hope that live inside you and are there to help you overcome and figure out everything in your life.

Can you relate to the grief and desperation? Well, it's time to make a change, choose the best, and start living every day like the world is just waiting to hear from you! God gave you free will to do just that.

You CAN get what you want, because you are ready to embrace extraordinary every single day. You are going to leave behind those thoughts of "wishing for something better" and look forward to creating your thriving business and life.

You can face all the challenges you will encounter when you get intentional about what matters most to you and why, for example, the reason you want to work from home or live in a different state or be with different people.

If you live a superficial life, your beliefs and values are going to be based on the latest trend and whatever grabs your attention. That kind of living scares me, and it should scare you, too!

Think about it—how can you get what you want for creating your thriving business and life when there is nothing to anchor you every day? You are being pushed in one direction then in another each time you spot some new viral video on how to look cool!

"What we know matters, but who we are matters more."

- Brené Brown

Being someone other than who you really are, which is your authentic self, is going to have you feeling an emptiness inside. You know what I'm talking about because you have felt it at some time in your life. AND, it was a sucky feeling, right?!

Alright, it's time to figure out what you want and become aware of the three keys for creating your thriving business and life.

Ready? Read on!!

Key #1

Ignite

What do you think about when you let yourself gaze out the window and daydream? Do you imagine being healthier, having a better relationship with someone, becoming a more positive person, or moving to a higher level with your business?

When you allow yourself to daydream, you are releasing the vision you desire to have. Here's my next question: do you believe you can make that a reality or do you leave it in the "hoping and wishing" box?

You have a spark inside you that glows brighter some days more than others. What if I told you that spark can grow and increase in intensity so much that people are going to start noticing and asking you "how do you have so much confidence and energy all the time?"

As I was walking through the airport after my last business conference, I saw a mom with two littles that were jumping up and down and running around. I looked at her (she was on a low level) and said, "Don't you wish you had one-tenth of their energy!" She laughed and said, "I sure do!"

There can be a correlation made between that scenario and your daily life with your business. You find yourself on a low level and yet all the needs of the day are just swirling around you, never slowing down.

When you can increase that glow inside you, that inner drive and direction, it's the gas you need to ignite your spark into flames.

Let me share another story with you. I love stories because they help me visualize just how I can apply them to my life!

In the back of my property there were several trees, and before the spring of the following year it was necessary to burn off all the leaves and old undergrowth. We would ignite one area and then the next to get the flame going so it could burn away all the unnecessary parts.

There was always a water hose nearby ready to tamp down the fire if it moved into an area we weren't ready for. And being a good neighbor, we knew this would add value to the neighborhood.

What does this have to do with your thriving business and life? There are three reasons:

1. Igniting different areas is important for your overall healthy growth.
2. Keeping focus on your overall goal is continual; it's not setting one fire and walking away.
3. With a plan and boundaries in place, the value you will add to your business and life will increase.

Get ready, because I am going to share how you can keep your internal flame ignited longer.

Lock #1
Responsibility

Can you think of an event, circumstance, or situation that didn't work out and now you struggle with trying again?

What I'm asking you might make you feel uncomfortable, because I want you to look back on your life and examine what you might be holding onto, still to this day, that is preventing you from having your thriving business and life.

Let's look at how your spark is being tamped down from your past.

I want you to think about this: Is there a situation that you feel you may have resolved but it rears its ugly head when you want to accomplish something new in your life? A new intention or a new goal?

Let me give you some examples to help you understand what you might need to be looking for:

1. You got in the best shape of your life, but slowly old eating habits crept back in and you started putting on more weight.
2. You were in a great relationship but over time you felt like that person didn't listen to you or love you like in the beginning, and that relationship ended.
3. You had to shut the doors on your business because it wasn't working after years of effort.

Today, when you want to get in shape or lose weight, your thoughts might be, *But I didn't continue with it last time. What if I do the same thing this time?*

Today, when you want to have a new relationship, your thoughts might be, *But I got hurt in the last one, so why do I think it would work now?*

Today, when a new business opportunity is presented, your thoughts might be, *But what if this time doesn't work either? I'm really going to feel like a failure.*

The story about burning the leaves and underbrush has some important analogies I want you to get:

1. The leaves and underbrush represent limiting beliefs, unresolved conflict, or critical thoughts concerning past missteps.

    a. Anything that is preventing you from attaining that thriving business and life needs to be removed and replaced.

2. The fire is removing the leaves and underbrush so that the area is cleared out and new growth can occur. New growth for you is:

    a. New goals
    b. New thoughts
    c. New actions

3. The water can serve as both a good and bad representation.

   a. The bad is your limiting beliefs, your doubt, your lack of structure, and lack of confidence tamping out your spark.

   b. The good is it forms boundaries that are needed in your life, so your flame burns brightest in your zone of genius (area or activity in which a person excels and experiences the highest level of creativity, productivity, and satisfaction.)

Now you are going to write down what is still occupying space in your brain and holding you back, then do three things:

1. Take responsibility for your part in it.
2. Forgive yourself for what happened.
3. Give yourself permission to try again as you celebrate the goal you have set.

It is so easy for you to be critical of yourself when NOW is the time to show self-care and self-respect to you. By doing this, you will become fully aware of what is holding you back and you can take measures to overcome that.

"When a woman becomes her own best friend, life is easier."

- Diane Von Furstenberg

Don't ever let a lesson be wasted.

   a. Examine it.
   b. Understand it.
   c. Learn from it.

Take the positive and leave the negative in the past. This awareness can be incredibly freeing for you. It brings to light some **Thing**, some **Action**, or some **Feeling** that has been hiding in the shadows.

You know that feeling you get when something feels off, just not right, but you can't put your finger on it?

Here's another example of what I'm talking about so you can see it clearer:

You are standing in a dark room and hear a strange sound, something that you can't quite figure out. No matter how hard you try, you just can't. The unease starts to creep in because the noise continues and you can't see what it is.

You look at your hand and you are holding a flashlight. All you need to do is ignite the light (flip the switch on). The light shines on your pet in the corner who is making noises in their sleep! You laugh because this was not a life-or-death situation. But until you acted—turned the flashlight on—you were paralyzed with fear (true story!).

Looking back at past missteps can be like this. It may not be fun (or even make you laugh), but in the scheme of things, the importance it holds becomes less as you are able to look realistically at what happened and how you can grow through it.

It's your responsibility to stand up for yourself but also be able to admit when something goes wrong, forgive yourself, give permission to try again, and commit to making corrections.

Three action words for you are:

  a. Responsibility

  b. Forgiveness

  c. Permission

Be accountable for your actions, they are yours, so own them. If you need to make the choice to change them, do it.

Lock #2
Vision Mapping

How great is it to know that you don't have to take eight or more hours every day, head down, working hard, to create the success you want?

Maybe it's the way my brain works, and maybe it's the way your brain works, but having the ability to take small actions every day and you see your efforts paying off makes us feel like we can accomplish anything!

James Clear, in his book *Atomic Habits*, shares this about one-percent action every day:

> "Meanwhile, improving by 1 percent isn't particularly notable—sometimes it isn't even noticeable—but it can be far more meaningful, especially in the long run. The difference a tiny improvement can make

over time is astounding. Here's how the math works out: if you can get 1 percent better each day for one year, you'll end up thirty-seven times better by the time you're done. Conversely, if you get 1 percent worse each day for one year, you'll decline nearly down to zero. What starts as a small win or a minor setback accumulates into something much more." (1)

How cool is that? Does this mean you don't have to spend hours upon hours working every day, giving up precious family time and much-needed sleep to be successful?

YES, IT DOES!

So how can you apply this new knowledge? Let's use it for your vision mapping success.

Vision mapping is an excellent way to write down your vision and make it plain. Here is another powerful scripture that gives you the instructions to do that:

Habakkuk 2:2-3 (AMP Bible)
"Write the vision
And make it plain on tablets,
That he may run who reads it.
Three For the vision is yet for an appointed time;
But at the end it will speak, and it will not lie.
Though it tarries, wait for it;
Because it will surely come,
It will not tarry."

Do you know what that means for you? It means that you have been given the

Instructions to write down your visions so that whoever reads it can run; so that you can read it and run; your team can read it and run; your family can read it and run.

And the vision is yet for an appointed time. You set a time when you want that vision to be completed. It may take a little while for you to accomplish what your vision is, but it will not tarry, it will surely come!

That is so empowering, because now is the time for your vision to become a reality and you to create your thriving business and life!

Your vision mapping is simple, and this is what it includes:

    a. Written goals

    b. Measurable tools

    c. Action steps

Your vision mapping will turn your vision into reality.

You need to be crystal clear about what you want, where you're heading, and how you'll get there.

Start by thinking of your overall vision that can be in 1 year, 2 years, 5 years, etc.

By putting a plan in motion, you will be able to celebrate when you reach your goal!

Do you mind if I share another story with you about doing this? Okay, great!

I grew up playing golf and really loved the game. It can be a mind game, so if you start having doubts about any part of your game, good grief, it really affects it!

My putting was usually something I never worried about, but then I got the yips! I would have that slight hesitation before my putting stroke, and it would throw off my putt every time! Okay, that just made me mad, and I decided I needed to take action, practice putting more, stay strong with my routine with each putt, and visualize it going in the hole.

Thinking about what was causing my hesitation with each shot, taking tiny actions to correct my misstep, and believing I could get my putting skills back is how I regained my confidence!

The next time I went out golfing, I birdied hole 9 and hole 18 at Diamondhead Golf Course in Hot Springs, Arkansas, which I had never done. It was a big goal for me, and did I celebrate that? You betcha!!

With your vision mapping, you can take the time to focus on the smaller milestones that will make up the bigger picture for creating your thriving business and life.

One of my clients shared that instead of making large goals and feeling bummed out when she didn't hit them, she chooses to focus on what step she needed to do on just that one day. By doing that, she felt like she had a win to carry her over to the next day.

The purpose of vision mapping is to help you clarify and focus on your goals, enhance motivation and inspiration, and visualize your desired outcomes. By creating a visual representation of your goals, you can better understand what you want, create a plan of action, and increase your chances of success.

"Success is the sum of small efforts repeated day in and day out."

- Robert Collier

After you have your long-term vision/goal, you need to create that more immediate goal and set an end date, which, you can break it down monthly. What is so awesome about the thirty days is you can set a beginning date even if it's the 16th of the month on a Wednesday. And don't forget to reward yourself for completing the goals, which will feel so amazing to you when you do!

By doing these things, it's going to help you stay focused, motivated, and energized toward your goals. It's a great way to keep track of your progress and massive success by working through the smaller action steps that you build to achieve your larger goals.

Vision mapping is all about having faith that what you want is achievable. Believe and trust in yourself, power through the difficult times, and never give up until you reach your vision destination. That is determination combined with perseverance.

Put one foot in front of the other, and keep going! Your future is in your own hands to make it happen! The only thing standing between where you are and where you want to be is YOU!

Now you understand that you matter and the choice is yours to start igniting different areas of your business and life so they can match your vision. So, let's look at your areas and get you creating your overall vision for success.

Your vision map is going to be the four core areas for creating your thriving business and life. I like to call this your C4 because it can be molded into any shape to change the direction of the resulting explosion—which is the direction you want to go for your thriving business and life.

Now is the time for you to change the direction of where your business and life are headed so that they can be ignited to the fullest strength!

Your Four Core Areas are:

1. Power – Health

2. Passion – Relationships

3. Purpose – Mindset

4. Production - Business

Power

Power is first, and it's all about your health! Your health is important for you to create your thriving business and life. It's a priority to make sure you have the right tools for success.

To be successful in business, your body needs enough energy so that all its cells can function optimally. Without this basic need met, not only will there always be some level of stress, but any opportunity at growth or development could slip away.

The key here isn't just doing "some" exercise but having a committed time every single day (or an x number of days) devoted exclusively to practicing healthy living habits.

Whether this looks like taking a jog or a walk in the morning, eating more greens and less processed foods, or investing in some quality supplements for optimal health; any of these can help ensure that you'll have enough energy to take on whatever your day throws at you—without having to worry about feeling drained or stressed out.

When you take the time to invest in yourself and prioritize your own health, you'll be setting yourself up for success in both your business and in life.

What does your overall vision for your health look like? Write it down.

Passion

Passion is the second Core Area and is about Relationships. Relationships should be a source of joy and comfort—not stress and anxiety.

Having the right relationships is a must to achieving your goals and dreams.

Drama-filled relationships are exhausting, so where is there a need to build up a relationship you have right now in your business or personal life?

Is it a relationship you want to have in your life? If it is, what can you do to boost that relationship? Do you need to be more present with someone and put down your phone or your laptop; do you need to make someone feel they are more important in your life; do you need to call someone more often so they know your relationship matters?

What does your overall vision for your relationships look like? Write it down.

Purpose

Purpose is the third Core Area. The purpose of life is to live your best possible version, and it all starts with a positive mindset.

I believe in God, and He provides the strength I need in all areas of my life; His love never fails me.

> Psalm 73:28 NJKV "But it is good for me to draw near to God; I have put my trust in the Lord God, That I may declare all Your works."

The spiritual aspect of life will help make this world feel less like an obstacle on your path toward happiness—and there are more opportunities for you if you take the time to look for them. To be able to clearly see the path before you, your mindset needs to be ignited toward confident living no matter what life is throwing your way.

I used to flower garden each year; replacing plants that were sickly with new ones, pruning the ones that were thriving so that they would grow even more, and taking care of the health of my garden.

With a quick once over, I could discover if anything needed more attention, but if I didn't keep an eye on it, problems could start getting bigger!

I love how nature can be such a great model for you and me! Whether you ever did any type of gardening, you have seen what a garden looks like, right?

If you compare sickly plants to your thoughts that aren't healthy, you can see why it's so important to remove them and replace them with healthy plants (thoughts). What you want to do is plant good seeds, flowers, etc. (positive thoughts and actions) and get rid of the weeds that can choke you to death.

Basically, you need to cultivate a healthy internal environment so that your outside environment can look the way you want it to. This can include prayer, meditation, affirmations, and positive journal prompts.

What does your overall vision for your mindset look like? Write it down.

Production

Production is your fourth Core Area, and the journey of production for your business starts where you are now, but it should also include a plan for the future.

This is because success in business doesn't just happen by chance or luck—there must be a purpose behind what actions are taken on any given day and on a weekly basis so that things can get better over time!

Here's a question for you: what is the ultimate goal for your business?

Get some clarity on who you want to serve, how big you want to grow, and how this will sustain your financial future.

One mentor told me years ago that if you treat your business like a hobby, it will pay you like a hobby. NOW is the time to figure out how important your business is to you!

Look at what you are doing right now. How important is your business success to you? Your actions should match your words here. If you dabble daily in your business but claim your business is very important so that you gain financial security, there's a disjointed relationship between your actions and your words.

Is your overall vision a "corner office with lots of windows," or do you see yourself stuck in "a cubicle" just getting through the day? Knowing what you want, believing you can get what you want, and implementing the actions will have you on your way to creating your thriving business and life.

What does your overall vision for your business look like? Write it down.

Lock #3
Non-Negotiable Actions

By structuring your day the right way, you are going to be able to get what you want for creating your thriving business and life. And it starts with intentional actions you take every day.

I really would like to take this one step further. Let me ask you; how many times do you catch yourself saying, "I intended to do that"? You say you are going to do something, you intend to do it, and then life happens. You get distracted, sidetracked, or just frustrated with the way the day is going.

This is where I take the words "intentional actions" and change them to "non-negotiable actions." This tells you that come hell or high water, you are going to get that action done! You might get side-swiped by events in your day, but you know beyond a shadow of a doubt that your "non-negotiable" is still going to get done.

How does having that kind of power make you feel? Pretty great, right?!

There have been so many times in your life that you felt helpless, so having a strategy to empower you is the key you are looking for in creating your thriving business and life.

Are you thinking, *Becky, what is a non-negotiable?* This looks different for you than it does for me. Let me share a couple of mine.

My morning rhythm (also called routine) is something I do every single day. It may be longer or shorter depending on the day and life situation, but I never let it go into the "I intended to do that" category.

My prayers and meditations on the day, my warm lemon water, my devotional, my high five in the mirror, my yoga stretch, and my journaling are going to happen no matter what.

When you care about how you interact with your daily life, relationships, and business, you will make that a non-negotiable action for yourself so that you will face each undertaking with positivity instead of negative reactivity.

Looking back on my "busy" lifestyle of being the feed store lady, raising three kids, and starting a "second chance" marriage with my soulmate, there wasn't a lot of goal setting, planning for success, or understanding what I even wanted.

You know what that's called? Surviving, not thriving!

As long as I was busy, jumping out of bed every day to begin the long list of tasks required for living, I thought everything must be right on track. But what was the purpose of it all?

Sure, I got the kids raised, continued running the feed store, and enjoyed life with my husband, but looking back, that was superficial living.

Superficial living is shallow living, not giving deeper meaning to what's important. This type of living reminds me of enjoying the moment without any thought of how today can impact tomorrow.

"I am aware that I am less than some people prefer me to be, but most people are unaware that I am so much more than what they see."

- Douglas Pagels

I didn't realize I had any non-negotiable actions in place. But one non-negotiable I did have was my prayer time. How can you even face trials and tribulations without faith in something bigger than yourself?

When you know your C4 in this stage of your life, because it will change over your lifetime, every action you take is either enriching it or eroding it. Getting real about what your choices are costing you can be a wake-up call!

Have you kept yourself busy every day, not giving much thought to how it was affecting the quality of your day or the quality of your future?

Looking closer at what is important to you and what you really want to achieve for yourself and your family is where your answer lies for creating your thriving business and life.

If you let one day flow into another day without any rhyme or reason, that emptiness will permeate your actions and your attitude every day. You were created for so much more than ordinary existence. You were created for extraordinary living!

NOW is the time to create your non-negotiable actions for your life and business.

The following is part of the non-negotiable actions you can embrace day to day for the success of your thriving business and life.

No matter what else you do in your morning rhythm to increase your momentum, DO NOT LOOK AT YOUR PHONE! You don't want to be drawn into the drama of other people's worlds;

you don't want to start influencing your brain negatively, which affects your emotions, which in turn affect your thoughts.

This is the time for you to use your creative thoughts to increase your power, passion, purpose, and production. You came up with your vision; what you want each of those areas to look like. You can use journal jotting, visualizing, and meditating on why it's important. What is your goal for thirty days, and what does your one step each day look like to reach that goal?

Do you realize the power that comes from creating your own tactical non-negotiable actions each day? Just stop and think about this. You create a small non-negotiable action you want to do today, then replicate that for tomorrow, then the next day, and so on.

This will become an action that is on autopilot, because it becomes part of you!

You can find your own copy of the Morning Rhythm infographic at:
www.3keys2getwhatyouwant.com/resources.

Once you get in the flow of a daily rhythm, it will be so much easier to start adding your C4 non-negotiable actions as they become part of the success for your business and life.

Key #2
Refine

Give yourself a high-five for grabbing your Key #1, igniting and opening your three locks of Responsibility, Vision Mapping, and Non-Negotiable Actions.

Ready to refine who you are and what you are doing? Great! Let's go!

It's time for the rebuild of you.

Refine means to remove impurities and to improve something by making small changes.

Let me ask you, are you the same person you were ten years ago? I bet you aren't. You've done a little refining along the way without even realizing that's what you were doing.

For example, when you were in your twenties (maybe thirties and forties), were Friday nights the time to go out with friends, maybe drink a little too much, just to do it again on Saturday nights?

That probably went on for several years until you realized you didn't have the stamina to keep doing that, and maybe you moved into a different relationship in your life and that lost its grip on you.

Maybe you didn't go to church after you hit adulthood because there were too many other fun things to do on the weekends and you really needed to sleep in.

With years comes maturity and an understanding that faith is the anchor to get you from one weekend to the next (especially with the societal craziness that exists today).

Do you see how you were refining yourself without seeing what was happening?

Now is the time to look at some deeper ways to refine yourself so that you can show up for that thriving business and life you are dreaming about.

"I choose to make the rest of my life the best of my life."

- **Louise Hay**

Have you ever done any renovation or remodeling of a home?

Have you ever known someone who renovates or remodels homes?

Have you ever seen a show where they are renovating or remodeling a home?

My husband and I loved watching the shows on HGTV of different folks who took a home that needed refining by repair, updating, or just making it fit the owner's new situation.

It inspired me to try my hand at renovating/redecorating my own home. Which area do you think I tried? Kitchen, oh that wasn't going to happen! Bedroom? I kind of liked that area.

It was the full guest bathroom that was still stuck in 1979! I picked out a new granite countertop, new sinks and fixtures, new mirror, and new toilet.

Now, you might ask me, was there a problem with the things in this bathroom that needed to be replaced?

Not necessarily, everything was still in working order, or as good as it could be. But I knew it could be better; not only aesthetically but functionally.

The toilet was blue, it must have been a "thing" in 1979. The inner workings

were constantly needing to be replaced. Upgrading it to an efficient, low-flow, comfort height, white toilet was the perfect replacement!

Faucets that were easy to turn on and off just made me happy! Isn't it interesting how you put up with "stuff" that works okay but not with ease?

Kind of like accepting less-than in your life, right?

So, after changing all the parts of the bathroom that were working so-so and looking dreary, it felt… great! I couldn't believe how good it felt to walk in there! AND everything worked exactly as it was supposed to!

Was this easy to do? No, it took effort! It took using my brain to figure out exactly what I wanted, to find the people to do the work the right way, which meant using my voice to express what I wanted and listening to the

advice of people who did this for a living.

As you look at your business and your life, do you see areas where you need to refine the way it looks and where it is working or not working?

You never stay in one place; you are either moving forward or moving backward. Now is the time to stop accepting less in your life, ignoring the parts that are just so-so, and instead look for ways to update and innovate your business and life.

Lock #1
Strength

What you have been doing has been okay, but you see certain areas of yourself and business that have been weakened through time. Sure, at one time you were that new build or newly renovated "home" with the current colors, fixtures, and flooring.

However, now the structure you once had in place and were excited to "live in" is no longer holding up to the integrity you want for your business and life.

There is a crack in the foundation of YOU that is jeopardizing the structure of YOU.

Looking at this is like a home that has a crack in the foundation, you know that if it isn't fixed, it will continue to weaken the structure. So, what do you need to do?

When I lived in SW Houston in Missouri City, we bought a new home in 1979. It was a sweet three bedroom two and a half bath home. It had a raised living room with a hearth and huge fireplace that was on one wall of the room.

After a few years, there was a huge crack that developed in the tile at the front door, which was adjacent to the living room. It kept getting bigger, and we knew we had to find out what was going on.

Low and behold, that huge fireplace was pulling the living room away from the rest of the house. This weakness in the structure of the house could have been ignored, hoping for the best. But that wasn't a very smart plan if we wanted to retain the value in this home we loved. That's when we hired a company to come and put piers in the ground around the living room to level it back up.

You see, in that area of Houston, the soil was called gumbo; you could dig into that soil and it would literally stick in a clump to your shovel. The weirdest soil I had ever seen!! It reacts a lot like a sponge, expanding as it soaks up and retains moisture, and in very hot, dry conditions, the gumbo clay shrinks and cracks.

This expansion and retraction of the soil as the weather changed put stress on our home's foundation.

The three things I want you to take away from this story:

1. Be aware of your foundation; keep an eye on the different areas in your business and life so that you can detect any cracks in your foundation before they get too large.
2. Know that you are valuable and need to invest in the help needed to strengthen your foundation.
3. The piers that you need installed to level up and strengthen your foundation are your core values.

Core values make up your foundation to ensure the strength you need for getting what you want for your thriving business and life.

I love using nature as an example for you, and a tree came to mind.

On the arboristnow.com website regarding the anatomy of a tree, it says "Trees having wood at their core are what makes them more resilient, helps give them their incredible lifespans and making its branches more suitable for artistic pruning" (2).

This means for you that your core values will increase your resiliency in dealing with adversities and opportunities, and by taking away the stress that comes with that, your lifespan will expand, along with your ability to stand firmly in your approach to your business and life.

I love that visual of comparing you to a tall and beautiful tree, which resonates with strength and endurance!

In identifying your core values, it's important to ask yourself what really matters in life and determine which values you prioritize.

When you have clarity about your values, it will be easier for both you and those around you (friends and family) to respect them as well as understand why they matter so much to you.

Knowing your core values can be incredibly beneficial in elevating both your life and business. Your core values reflect who you are, how you act, and what you stand for.

Here are four key benefits to knowing your core values:

1. Increased Self-Awareness: being able to identify and understand your own personal core values will help provide clarity on who you really want to be as a person and what areas of life need the most work or development. This self-awareness can lead to improved decision making, commitment, and dedication toward achieving desired goals.

2. Improved Focus: Being aware of your core values allows you to focus your efforts on things that truly matter to you instead of randomly pursuing objectives which have less meaning or no long-term value at all. Know-

ing your true purpose helps you live an authentic life with greater fulfillment and joy from within!

3. More Resiliency: Knowing your core values gives you the strength you need when facing challenging times or difficult decisions, as it helps ground you in your identity by reminding you why you do the things that you do rather than being influenced by external pressures or opinions which may not always serve you in the best way.

4. Greater Inspiration: Finally, knowing what you really want helps you come up with creative ideas that can help you reach those goals. These ideas come from things that have meaning to you, which increases your chances of success.

To get started on understanding these underlying levels of awareness regarding yourself, consider trying some exercises like mindfulness meditation or journaling focused solely on who you are deep down inside; these strategies allow for deeper levels of exploration into why certain activities make YOU feel good versus others.

Another real-life example was from a gal I follow online, Joan Jakel, on her blog post about using your voice to stay in integrity with your core values.

Joan went to a pharmacy to get medication for her pet. As she sat in the other lane, she witnessed the exchange between the pharmacist and another customer who was explaining that their phone system was not working. Unfortunately, the pharmacist took that as a personal insult and told the customer that she was wrong and basically bullied her into submission.

Well, Joan had experienced the same problem with the phone system. After taking in this exchange that ended with the customer feeling browbeaten, Joan checked within herself for what her authentic response was going to be. She shared with the pharmacist that she experienced the same problem with their phone system.

The pharmacist started to argue with Joan and Joan politely stopped her. Joan told her she can choose what she wants to do with the information, and the appropriate response to a customer who is trying to help with a perceived business issue is to simply say "thank you." But the pharmacist started to stammer, and Joan stopped her again.

Joan very calmly and firmly said, "You're only response is to say, 'Thank you for the feedback.'" She stopped and took it in. Finally, the pharmacist said, "Thank you," calmed down, and then politely assisted Joan.

Joan said if she had not spoken up, she would have regretted it. It would have chipped away at her integrity by not honoring her core values (which include authenticity, courage, love, and spirituality, which is defined by her as "concerned with the human spirit or soul"). Joan hoped the pharmacist would think twice about how she responds to, and treats, customers in the future (3).

Here are five key core values that would be worth you investing time exploring further; integrity, ambition, adventure/curiosity, compassion, kindness, and humility—all essential traits needed during your journey through life, no matter where it might take you!

You can find the Core Values sheet in the bonus area at: www.3keys2getwhatyouwant.com/resources.

Having a clear understanding of your core values can help you make better decisions, remain focused on your goals, propel yourself to get what you want, and lead a more meaningful life.

Lock #2
Stance

What is your power center? You know, your load-bearing structural pillars. Those attributes that will keep you grounded and secure.

There is a four-by-five-foot opening, not the doorway, between the kitchen and dining room in my house. It's like a window opening inside the house but without glass in it. It's hard to explain so that you can get a visual, because I couldn't figure out why the builders put it there. Until I understood that they wanted it to be open between the kitchen and the dining room, but because that opening would be too wide, there needed to be a load-bearing pillar. The owners ended up hanging a large stained glass in this opening (but with the three little kids that I had, that was a bad idea!!)

Anyway, for the structural integrity of what the builders were wanting to do, there had to be a load-bearing pillar (I guess that was before they made load bearing beams that went up in the ceiling).

The purpose of this structural pillar is to distribute the weight properly from one area to another.

For your stance, there are three pillars that need to be installed in your business and life:

1. Your voice
2. Your boundaries
3. Your faith

"Forget mistakes. Forget failure. Forget everything except what you're going to do now and do it."

- Will Durant

Pillar #1 - Your Voice

Pillar #1 is developing the power of your voice, which is essential for making yourself understood and expressing what you want. Learning to communicate effectively can help pave a path toward achieving your goals.

I came up with the Five Bs to develop your voice:

1. Be Concise: Think about what it is you really want. You must know what that is so that the other person understands. Keep it simple and to the point.

2. Be Precise: People are not mind-readers, even when you think they should be! If you need time to do something, let it be known. If you need help with a task, ask for it. Give all the required information for others to understand.

3. Be Accessible: Having the courage to express your needs is essential, but it's equally important to remain approachable and open minded with eye contact, a relaxed body, and the right tone.

4. Be Aware: This applies to not only speaking up but being present to hear what is being said to you. Present means being in the moment, not three steps ahead.
5. Be Observant: Look for others who are good communicators that you are attracted to and model them.

Your words, your tone, and your body language all come into play when you know the outcome you are wanting.

Just visualize yourself as that calm, cool, and collected woman you want to be! You can feel that secure and confident emotion rise out of your being because you know your five B's!

Pillar #2 - Your Boundaries

Just as you would have a fence around your backyard (your boundary) to keep people or animals out, you need to set personal boundaries. I mean who wants someone or something to just come through your yard willy-nilly!

Creating boundaries in your life and business is an essential part of living a productive, healthy lifestyle. Boundaries not only help you stay organized and focused but also create a positive environment for both you and those around you. (Remember your fence!)

Here are five ways to create boundaries in your business and life:

1. Know Your Limits: It's important to be aware of what you can realistically handle in terms of the amount of work you take on, the number of hours that you spend working, or the commitments that you make. Knowing your limits ensures that you don't overextend yourself when dealing with the plethora of tasks or projects that can happen.

    How many times have you said yes to doing something only to regret it? You found out that you were saying yes to added stress and strain on your business and life.

    Remember the importance of setting specific goals for yourself as well as limiting activities or meetings outside of core working hours—this will keep distractions at bay while also allowing time for restorative breaks throughout the day (and who doesn't need those restorative breaks!).

2. Delegate Responsibilities: Learning to delegate responsibilities is one of the most crucial strategies when it comes to creating effective boundaries within your business or home environment. If something isn't directly related to your job function or personal goals, don't hesitate to ask someone else who may be more qualified or better equipped than you are. This way, tasks can get done quicker and efficiently while freeing up extra space for other opportunities you could invest your energy into.

Here is a huge question for you: Do you feel like you are the ONLY person who can do everything in your business and life? Think about it; it may sting when you see what type of environment you have created by thinking you are the end-all to all things in your life.

3. Show Gratitude & Appreciation: It's important to show gratitude toward others who pick up tasks when it's needed and provide support throughout any project-related endeavors; this helps build strong relationships among team members and family members based on mutual respect and understanding. When everyone gets along well with each other because of showing appreciation toward each other's efforts, operations run smoother from start till finish (I always say everyone wants to feel appreciated, and sometimes you must give that other person the opportunity to serve you).

4. Establish Emotional Boundaries: When it comes to creating boundaries, it's important to have emotional intelligence. Our emotions can often act as signals when something isn't right or if we're getting taken advantage of.

    By taking the time to reflect on how you are feeling in any given situation, you can identify strong emotional triggers, which will help you know when it's time to draw a line in the sand and protect yourself from being taken advantage of (remember to NOT tell yourself a story about what you THINK is going on instead of what the reality may actually be).

5. Say No to What Doesn't Align with Your Goals: You can often find yourself saying yes even when you don't want to because you don't feel comfortable saying no due to fear or guilt; however, this often leads you down paths that won't take you to where you want to go. This will ultimately end in wasted energy and resources along with unfulfilled goals and intentions (your non-negotiable actions). Instead, speaking up and expressing what doesn't align with your own personal goals will allow you to retain better control over situations, keeping focus on your progress instead of regretting missing opportunities later down the line.

Altogether, creating proper boundary conditions helps bring about greater balance in both physical and emotional aspects, allowing you more clarity and freedom while helping keep meaningful relationships intact. Doing this helps allow more peace and productivity into your life, which paves the way toward healthier living habits and successful outcomes to get what you want across all areas of your thriving business and life!

Pillar #3 - Your Faith

When I am relying on my ego to gain success, the "I CAN DO THIS," it feels like a struggle, and the end result is not what I had hoped for. When I'm relying on listening to God's nudging, asking for His help, and being receptive is when the actions flow, success follows.

"Trust in the Lord with all your heart; do not depend on your own understanding. Seek his will in all you do, and he will show you which path to take."

- Proverbs 3:5-6 NLT

This is not where I try to evangelize you and get you to agree with me. This is where you will be exposed to other possibilities that you may not have thought about before.

Don't decide that you will skip this part because it doesn't apply to you. Keep an open mind and see what might resonate with you for your success.

Make Faith an Essential Part of Your Decision-Making Process

When it comes to making difficult decisions in your business, faith can play a large role in keeping you on the right path. Whenever you are faced with a challenging decision, take the time to consider the potential impact that faith could have on the outcome. Pray for guidance and use wisdom in determining what is best for you and your business. Making faith a part of your decision-making process can provide much needed clarity and peace of mind when facing tough choices.

Follow Your Intuition

We all have an inner "knowing" that will guide us if we pay attention to it. This inner knowing is your intuition, and it's one way God speaks to you about various situations or decisions you must make in life or business. Trusting this intuition requires practice, and if you listen to it, you will find it incredibly beneficial, as you're more likely to make informed decisions that lead you closer to your goals instead of distracting you from your ultimate mission in life and business.

Become Unshakeable in Difficult Times

When times get tough, having faith can provide you with emotional stamina like no other emotion out there; allowing you to tap into inner strength even when things seem insurmountable. It's important to nurture resilience by being clear about any doubts or fears. Then cultivating a deeper trust through prayerful meditation and connecting with your higher power will help transform any overwhelmed feelings into a peaceful assurance, which provides long term security no matter what is going on around you.

By keeping faith at the center of your business and life, you'll be able to find more joy and fulfillment in whatever work you do. Faith provides a foundation for success, as it allows you to trust in God's plans for your life, even if you don't know what that looks like yet.

Lock #3
Stability

When it comes to building stability for yourself and your business, surrounding yourself with the people who will help you stay grounded is essential. It's important to recognize that not just anyone can contribute positively to your life and pursuits, but rather individuals who have qualities such as trustworthiness, empathy, and accountability; these are all key traits of stable relationships.

Trustworthiness is paramount when forming strong bonds. This means putting faith in one another and being honest with each other. Accentuating this trait will solidify the foundation of any relationship. It also involves respecting boundaries—understanding each other's needs without crossing lines or straying outside acceptable boundaries for both parties involved.

Empathy is essential when building meaningful relationships, as it enables you to understand how someone else feels in order to build a deep connection which has a high chance of lasting long-term. This entails truly listening and responding appropriately while having an open mind toward their perspectives.

Accountability builds responsibility within relationships so that you can rely on one another knowing that you won't let each other down or leave anyone in a disadvantaged position if something were to happen unexpectedly or challenges arise along the way. Through accountability you will keep expectations realistic yet achievable while staying committed even through adversity. Creating stability within relationships while you keep moving forward together toward common goals, despite any challenges which may come up throughout the process, will culminate in an ultra-successful path overall.

Ultimately, by investing time into cultivating meaningful relationships with people who value similar principles like trustworthiness, empathy, and accountability, you can foster sustainable relationships within your life, effectively nurturing and enhancing your quest for ongoing success no matter what obstacles come your way.

Building stability through the people you surround yourself with is an essential part of achieving success in both business and life. Your network of friends, colleagues, and mentors can be a powerful asset to your personal growth as well as the growth of any organization or project you are involved in. To harness this power, it is important to focus on creating relationships founded on mutual trust and respect.

I have been so blessed to have those key people in my life at just the right time. However, if I had kept myself closed off, afraid to be vulnerable, then I would have missed these incredible opportunities to be with just the right people I needed in the different chapters of my life.

When it comes to building stability through the people you surround yourself with for your business or other professional activities, there are several strategies that may be beneficial. I want you to consider investing energy into networking events geared toward meeting ambitious professionals just like you who share similar values and goals.

These events can help create valuable relationships that allow for mentorship, knowledge exchange, or collaborative projects down the road. Additionally, take advantage of social media platforms such as LinkedIn, Facebook, and Instagram, which offer opportunities to connect with individuals from all over the world who bring different experiences and expertise to the table.

The friends I have across the United States and the rest of the world means so much to me personally and professionally! If these relationships depended on me being physically in their home, my world would have shrunk tremendously.

By selecting peers who have complementary goals that align with yours—versus those simply wanting to use you as a steppingstone to their own success—you'll find greater stability long-term within your professional circle, which can result in countless possibilities for success down the road.

On a personal level, relationships based on positive reinforcement rather than competition play an equally crucial role when it comes to creating inner peace (and external success). Whether these come in the form of family members, close friends, or even acquaintances, embrace those connections by making them mutually beneficial so that everyone stays focused on understanding each other instead of competing against each other.

Feeling better about yourself and feeling more like a part of a support system will make you much more confident personally and professionally.

Key #3

Evaluate

You must be feeling great at this point in your journey through the keys and locks! Remember, the point in starting to add positive actions to your business and life is to get the momentum going for you, one step at a time.

When it comes to evaluating your actions and determining if they are working or need to be changed, there are a few key elements to consider. Both in terms of business success and personal life fulfillment, understanding how you can make yourself more effective is key!

One way to determine your effectiveness is to do an honest evaluation of where you are currently with your actions:

Are they driving the desired results?

How could they be improved?

What kinds of changes could help increase effectiveness?

Think critically about these questions before deciding whether a change of plan is needed. By taking the time to evaluate how successful your current actions are, you can create benchmarks for improvement.

I want you to think about "busy" people you know (and you may be one of them). You know the type, always staying busy where one day just flows into another and not much gets accomplished. BUT that person is ALWAYS busy!

My feed store days were filled with days like this. Not only was I running a business, but I also had kids' activities to go to, helping my husband in his business, and community obligations I was a part of.

I felt that if I was busy, I must be valuable to someone or something else. I never stopped to evaluate what was working and what wasn't regarding my overall growth and well-being. My goals weren't being set, so they were never going to be reached, were they?

It's also important to seek feedback from other sources, such as customers or colleagues, brainstorming with your inner circle who you trust and who can provide valuable information on what's worked well and where improvements could be made going forward.

This is why you need to evaluate what you're doing and what you have in place for your success, getting what you want for your thriving business and life. All of this will provide valuable information on what works best for your circumstances when you need to make those improvements going forward.

Lock #1
The Pivot

Understanding the power of the pivot is incredibly important when evaluating what's working and what isn't in your business and life. A pivot means to make a change or adjust your course of action, sometimes dramatically, in response to a change in your circumstances or some newfound information. The pivot can be an opportunity disguised as a setback.

Read that sentence again: "The pivot can be an opportunity disguised as a setback."

You know your first reaction to something that isn't working the way you wanted it to can be a negative reaction, and one that you direct at yourself as the one to blame. Go back to your letter and the first Key Responsibility to remind yourself that you are not going to play the blame game!

You had a part in it and now you need to pivot, but what a great learning experience for you to remember for the future when you feel a pivot coming again.

Gaining experience is your best defense against struggles you might run into, because now you know what to do next.

Pivoting helps you to be flexible and creative when something changes. You don't have to start over from the beginning every time. You can look at your plan again with new information or ideas and make changes without starting from scratch.

When you understand how powerful this tool is, it allows you to build resilience within your business while always ensuring growth—no matter if things are going well or taking a downturn due to outside forces **beyond your control**.

Pivoting is an essential skill for both business and life that can help you get to where you want to go. Knowing when to pivot, the key strategies for understanding the why behind it, and how best to do it can dramatically increase your chances of success.

"Forces beyond your control can take away everything you possess except one thing; your freedom to choose how you will respond to the situation."

- Victor Frankl

Here are three important strategies for better understanding why a pivot is important:

1. Understand Your Situation - Pivoting requires you to take a step back and evaluate your current situation. By getting clear on what's happening in your business or life right now, you can begin to identify potential challenges that might require you to make changes to progress further. Asking yourself questions such as "What am I working toward?" or "What could be improved upon?"

will give you the insight you need on when a pivot may be necessary.

2. Identify Weaknesses & Strengths - Once you have clarity on your current state, it's then important to understand both weaknesses and strengths that exist within it which could potentially determine an upcoming pivotal decision. Evaluating these two factors objectively will give you greater insight into where pivots should happen for improvement or growth opportunities not just today but also down the road, too.

3. Plan Ahead & Anticipate Potential Issues - There will always be potential issues associated with any major pivot no matter how much thought has gone into planning it out beforehand; however, proactively thinking through possible scenarios before implementing a pivot helps reduce risk factors substantially!

When you are planning something, think about what might go wrong. If something doesn't work out the way it's supposed to, plan for how you will fix it. This way, if something bad happens, you can act quickly and fix the problem.

Using these three strategies can help you make good decisions when things change. You can adjust your plans so that you don't miss any chances and use all the information in the right way.

The pivot can show up in small ways or big ways. An example of a big way is when my feed store was losing money month after month. Pivoting to a whole new venture scared me to death, but the impending doom of this business I loved scared me more! So much so that within thirty days I planned, carried it out, and closed my brick-and-mortar store! That was an "in your face" kind of pivot that could not be ignored!

Evaluating the financials and local economy gave me the answers I didn't want to see, but there was no denying them. It was time to pivot, set new goals for the next chapter, and put on my "big girl pants" to get it started. Pivoting doesn't mean the end of one thing has to be the end of all things. It just gives you the opportunity to make note of what worked and what didn't so that you can continue moving forward.

A small pivot can be something like when I was selling a "new puppy bundle" that I just loved so much but the time to create it was greater than the income from it. Yes, this was one of my products that I sent in as a seller with the fulfillment by Amazon program. I had painstakingly found each of the products in the bundle and lovingly put it together for new puppy owners, only to realize I had to let it go! I had to pivot to other products that had a higher profit margin and were not as labor intensive.

By developing the habit where you understand and value pivoting as an essential way for you to keep your forward momentum going, you will become a decision-maker better equipped with knowing that you need to be strategic in your planning. What will stop is you having to do a knee-jerk reaction because something has caught you by surprise.

What this means for you is an understanding of how vital it can be when you assess whether something is successful or not. Knowing if something is or isn't working means you can do things better. This will help you in your business and your life. You will be faster and smarter when trying new things because you don't have to start over every time.

I mention not having to start from scratch again because when you have your strategies in place for building on, you will never start from zero when you need to pivot. Why? Because you will take with you the framework for strategic growth and the confidence to keep moving toward your goals.

Lock #2
Accountability

You were created to be able to connect with other people. How successful were you on your health journey? Did you create the consistency with it that you thought you could? The same thing applies to your relationships, mindset, and business.

Maybe you associate accountability with the words you heard growing up: "Wait until your father (or mother) gets home! Then you're going to get it!" You were supposed to do something and didn't, so now you are going to have to pay for that.

It's easy to apply that same blame game to yourself when you try and try to accomplish something, alone, and it doesn't get done. Someone has to pay, and that person is usually YOU!

You cannot be an island unto yourself. Without the people and resources to make your next endeavor work the way you want it to, you will flail and overburden yourself. When you realize this, thinking about accountability takes on a whole new meaning. Incorporating accountability into your business and life is not meant to be a punishment; it's for your success!

Wow! How great does that feel?!

"Accountability is the bridge that will take you from where you are to where you want to be."

- Rebecca C Wilcox

While having a coach, mentor, teacher, or friend in your corner will help you stay on course, there are other ways you can create a success path with what you do.

Creating accountability and sticking to your goals can be a challenge, so time blocking and setting daily intentions are essential elements of success. Having a plan and taking the time to set clear objectives can help you stay on track and be more productive throughout each day.

Time blocking is an effective way to manage tasks efficiently by giving specific chunks of time for each activity. For example, you might block off ten to fifteen minutes in the morning for creative brainstorming, take a break at noon with some stretching or meditation, have an hour dedicated to writing emails, a blog post, or your book in the afternoon, etc.

Get a copy of your Time Success planner at www.3keys2getwhatyouwant.com/resources

This type of schedule allows you to focus on one task at a time without distractions from other obligations and tasks that require your attention throughout the day. It also helps avoid burn-out because it forces you to prioritize what needs immediate action versus long-term projects that may not need constant attention.

A word of warning: don't try to time block every minute of your day! The first time I started time blocking, I filled in the entire day! But guess what I forgot to schedule? Bathroom breaks, a lunch break, get up and move breaks! You get the picture!

One thing I saw from the clients I have coached is they had better focus, got more done, and didn't feel so overwhelmed because the most important tasks got done. You know how at the end of your day you wonder what you accomplished but you know you were busy all day long? You are going to start feeling so much better and more confident when you can look and see what you accomplished because you blocked out the time.

One of the biggest obstacles that you are going to eliminate are distractions that sidetrack you from what you really want to be doing. Distractions will always win out when you just willy-nilly go about your day without any direction. Discouragement will set in because you aren't making the progress you thought you would, and you don't understand why.

In addition to having an organized schedule with blocked-off times for activities, along with your non-negotiable actions, it's also important that you set daily intentions as part of your productivity strategy. Intention setting gives you clarity about your purpose behind what you do every day.

Setting daily intentions helps you keep focus on what needs to be done—and why those things need to get done—for the day ahead. Your work environment needs to be set up for maximum productivity. Make sure your tasks are organized in order of priority. Determining how much time should be spent on each task and balancing personal responsibilities requires dedication and commitment from within yourself first before anything else can happen externally.

To do this effectively requires understanding what exactly it is you want your end result (i.e., goal) to be in both business/career and life contexts; this means understanding the reasons behind why certain decisions you make have priority over other decisions.

If you have been doing the actions you read this book, you know your core values and you know your goals. Daily means every day, and intention means putting your focus and energy behind what you have set up for your day.

It's your way of being responsible for what you are doing in a positive way. Bring joy to everything you do, and your joy will begin to overflow in all areas of your business and life. This is just another way of creating your thriving business and life.

Your goals support your motivation, which leads to productivity. Therefore, when starting something new, make sure your intention is clear so that you can ultimately get more done!

Having intention-setting practices such as journaling or reflection exercises will help you know what might trigger stress before it is too late. This will help you keep doing the things that are important to you and have balance in your business and life.

Overall, creating accountability through time blocking, setting daily intentions, having your non-negotiable actions, journaling, and reflection provides structure within your business and life as well as providing mental clarity and health benefits when cultivated regularly—leading you closer to achieving optimal results in your life!

Lock #3
Celebration

Celebrations are a great way to recognize your accomplishments and show appreciation for the hard work and effort that went into reaching your goals. Celebrations can also be a powerful tool for motivation, inspiring you to keep striving for bigger and better successes.

In business, celebrations are powerful tools for improving performance. They can serve as incentives for you to achieve specific objectives. Celebrations motivate you and your team to work together toward common goals.

Celebrations create opportunities for fun while also providing chances to evaluate lessons you have learned or strategies you have adopted along the way. Studies have proven that when you and/or employees feel appreciated through celebration of achievements, it leads to higher productivity levels and greater involvement in your business initiatives.

Celebrations also bring beneficial effects into your personal life by reminding you how far you've come. When you do something good, it is important to recognize it. Even if it seems small, it is still important. This will help you stay positive when things don't go the way you want them to.

Think about all the celebrations you have had or been a part of in your life. There are graduation celebrations, wedding celebrations, baby celebrations, vacation celebrations, holiday celebrations, etc. You get the picture!

Celebrating wins, both big and small, is essential for personal growth and success in business and life. It motivates you to keep striving for your goals, shows appreciation for the hard work that went into achieving a goal, and helps foster an environment of collaboration.

Here are five strategies you can use to increase your ability to celebrate wins no matter how big or small:

1. Acknowledge accomplishments: Take time each day or even once a week to sit down with yourself and acknowledge any recent successes; this could be as simple as reflecting on something small like completing a task on time or creating a quick accomplishment such as writing blog posts.

   Every evening, I commit to writing in my journal at least three wins I had that day. You would be surprised how quickly you can overlook something as a win! You might be able to do this only once a week, but I can promise you I would not remember half of my wins if I didn't record them every day.

2. Focus on what worked: Instead of catastrophizing any mistakes that were made, focus on what went right during any project or task and use that knowledge for your future success. This gives you something positive yet realistic you can build on for future projects!

It took me several years to stop focusing on what went wrong when I had to close my brick-and-mortar store. By shifting my focus, evaluating what did work and how I was able to pivot, I was finally able to celebrate the courage and strength it took to do what I had to do!

3. Reward yourself with something tangible: Treating yourself provides incentive, but make sure it's not extravagant—buy something meaningful but affordable for you, like maybe going out to dinner at your favorite restaurant with friends/family once a goal has been met. Alternatively, save up toward bigger rewards over time such as vacations or other experiences once several goals have been met instead!

This was something I had not heard about until 3 years ago. Once I did this, I bought myself something to remind me of the success I had in my coaching business. I couldn't get over the immense pride it created because of what the item represented! I bought an Oura ring to monitor my sleep and exercise, just to name a few of its benefits. The ring not only reminds me of what I accomplished but encourages me to meet my next goals again and again!

4. Embrace self-compassion and mistakes as part of the journey: It goes without saying that you cannot achieve perfection, but if mistakes are seen more positively, then they can become part of the winning process! Instead of dwelling on missteps, use self-compassion techniques such as mindful reframing techniques (e.g., 'I did my best,' etc.) so that even wrong decisions become part of the learning journey rather than sticking points during failure! By embracing this attitude, every challenge becomes less daunting and will increase your motivation levels, further leading you toward greater celebrations!

5. Make celebration part of your routine: Make it a habit of celebrating your successes. Take some time at least twice a month to reflect on all that you've accomplished as you are working on your non-negotiable actions toward your thirty-day goals, no matter how small or

insignificant it may seem. This can become a celebration ritual for you that you can look forward to, plus it will continue to propel you forward toward your thriving business and life!

Overall, evaluating and celebrating accomplishments not only serves a practical purpose but also has psychological benefits too—it can help raise self-esteem levels through encouragement and recognition at crucial times along your journey toward getting what you want!

"A beautiful life will bloom from a beautiful mind that is nurtured by beautiful thoughts."

- **Dodinsky**

One Last Message

Imagine living a life of purpose, growth, and success—the kind that leaves you fulfilled and thriving. It's not a distant dream but a reality within your grasp. It all starts with the efforts you take, the people you interact with, and the way you embrace growth.

No more stagnation or suspended animation. Just like plants awaken from hibernation, you too can break free from dormancy and step into your full potential. The time for preparation is now, so you can seize opportunities when they arise.

It's time to act and achieve the results you desire. Just as physical movement gets your blood flowing, pursuing your thriving business and life propels you forward.

Unlock the three keys—Ignite, Refine, Evaluate—and witness the magic unfold. By understanding why your dreams matter, creating actionable steps, and consistently moving in the right direction, you'll open doors to the life you've always envisioned.

If you want something more for your business and life, you don't want to be overwhelmed with all you need to do, and you want ten-plus hours back each week, you will discover how to do this in my group program "Time Hack Fast Track Accelerator Program – Achieve Your Desired Goals with Ease While Unlocking MORE Time for your Family and Life!" at www.timehackfasttrack.com.

"Give yourself permission to imagine the different possibilities you could create for your life."

- Rebecca C Wilcox

Special <u>FREE</u> Bonus Gift for You!

To help you achieve more success, there are **FREE BONUS RESOURCES FOR YOU** at:

www.FreeGiftFromRebecca.com

About Rebecca Wilcox

Rebecca Wilcox is a Results Life Coach for faith-filled women who are undergoing significant changes. She offers tools and strategies to support her clients in stepping into their new chapter with clarity and confidence. Rebecca has coached women through life transitions such as divorce, career changes, moves, motherhood, retirement, and more.

Rebecca understands about making difficult decisions for which there's no clear or easy path. She specializes in coaching her clients to clarify their dreams, desires, goals, values, and priorities. Through her coaching, these women become more authentic, and achieving at a level they never imagined possible!

Rebecca has filmed over 300 #BeckyBite videos, been interviewed countless times in online communities and on podcasts and been a speaker on Virtual Summits sharing her wisdom about consistent habits for empowered living.

Rebecca graduated from the University of Arkansas and is coaching certified from Life on Fire Academy. Rebecca has been married since 1998 to her best friend. They have four children. She is the proud "Nonna" to seven grandchildren who light up her life.

At the time of this publication, Rebecca is currently accepting coaching clients in her Courageous Living program. She can be reached via the contact form at: www.rebeccacwilcox.com

Time Hack Fast Track Accelerator Program

- Achieve Your Desired Goals with Ease, While Unlocking MORE Time for Your Family and Life!

- 8 Week Program to Increase Your Time Freedom, Eliminate Guilt and Tackle Distractions Guaranteed

To invest in your future success, go to www.TimeHackFastTrack.com

References

(1) Clear, James; Author of Atomic Habits; 2018

(2) https://www.arboristnow.com/news/The-Basic-Anatomy-of-a-Tree; June 15, 2017

(3) Jakel, Joan; Blogger 'I'm Joan Jakel'; https://www.joanjakel.com/how-to-effectively-and-powerfully-use-your-voice/ ; May 25, 2022